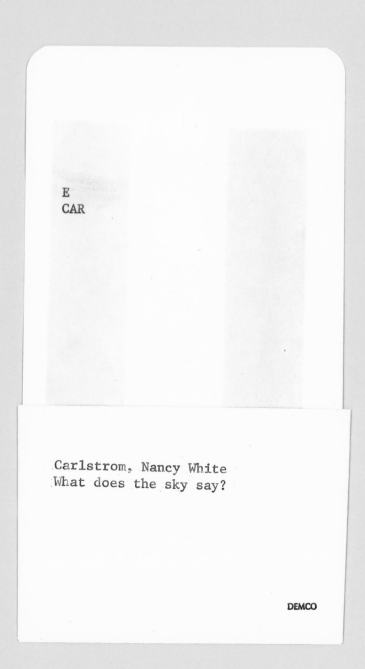

E
CAR

Carlstrom, Nancy White
What does the sky say?

DEMCO

Written by Nancy White Carlstrom
Illustrated by Tim Ladwig

EERDMANS BOOKS FOR YOUNG READERS

Grand Rapids, Michigan / Cambridge, U.K.

Text copyright 2001 by Nancy White Carlstrom
Illustration copyright 2001 by Tim Ladwig
Published 2001 by Eerdmans Books for Young Readers
An Imprint of Wm. B. Eerdmans Publishing Co.
255 Jefferson Ave. SE, Grand Rapids, Michigan 49503
P.O. Box 103, Cambridge CB3 9PU U.K.
www.eerdmans.com/youngreaders
Printed in Hong Kong
07 06 05 04 03 02 01   7 6 5 4 3 2 1
The scripture quotation is taken from the Holy Bible, New International Version®. NIV®.
Copyright©1973,1978,1984 by International Bible Society.
Used by permission of Zondervan Publishing House.

Library of Congress Cataloging-in-Publication Data

Carlstrom, Nancy White
    What does the sky say? / written by Nancy White Carlstrom;
        illustrated by Tim Ladwig
    p. cm.
    ISBN 0-8028-5208-4 (hardcover : alk.paper)
    1. Nature–Religious aspects–Juvenile literature.
    [1. Nature–Religious aspects.]
    I. Ladwig, Tim. ill. II. Title.

BT695.5 C365 2000
242'.62–dc21
                    00-056010

The illustrations were done in watercolor, pastel, and
    liquid acrylics on 140# Arches cold press paper.
The text type was set in Cheltenham.
The display type was set in President.
The book was designed by Gayle Brown.

For the Mitchell Family
Grayce, Rob, Carrie, and Emily
— *N. W. C.*

For Leah
— *T. L.*

What does the sky say on a winter day, when snow is falling and a mother is calling her little girl to dinner?

The sky says, "Remember. Go in
and be fed and loved, but don't forget
to look out the window."

The little girl makes big footprints
right up to her front door, and in the
morning she always looks out the window.
She does not mind that her tracks are covered,
for she sees the sparkling coat the sky left for her
snowman.

What does the sky say on a Saturday night before going out with the mountains in orange silk?

The sky says, "Dance, and don't look down at your feet."

The little girl twirls around and around until she is dizzy.

What does the sky say when the rain beats on its chest and the little girl cries because her best sand castle is ruined?

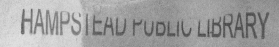

The sky says, "Look up! The sun is coming back.
See what a beautiful picture we can paint together."

The little girl looks up and sees colors.

What does the sky say when the leaves are blowing
and the geese going south?

The sky says, "Sing and you will always find your way home."

The little girl leans into the wind and does not feel lonely.

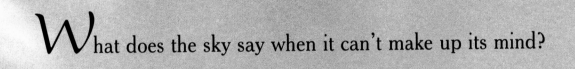

What does the sky say when it can't make up its mind?

The sky says, "Take a chance anyway."

The little girl comes home with wet socks and shoes and skinned knees, but that is the day she learns to ride a bike.

What does the sky say when its mouth is full of moon and its words are silenced with all that light?

It stretches out arms in sleeves of dark blue velvet and talks with its hands. And though it takes more than ears to hear such words, the sky says, "Listen. Listen to this bright shining earth! With such a fine wide roof I give you, surely there is room for everyone to live in peace."

The little girl hears with her heart
and knows that what the sky says is true.

And when she is old she will look up and say,
"I still believe. Don't you?"

And the sky, joining its voice with the many
others, will whisper, "Yes."

The heavens declare the glory of God;
the skies proclaim the work of God's hands.
Day after day they pour forth speech;
night after night they display knowledge.
There is no speech or language
where their voice is not heard.
Their voice goes out into all the earth,
their words to the ends of the world.

Psalm 19:1-4a